DATE DUE

JOSEPH MIDTHUN SAMUEL HITI

BUILDING BLOCKS OF SCIENCE

a Scott Fetzer company
Chicago
www.worldbook.com

World Book, Inc.
180 North LaSalle Street
Suite 900
Chicago, Illinois 60601
USA

For information about other World Book publications, visit our website at www.worldbook.com or call 1-800-WORLDBK (967-5325).
For information about sales to schools and libraries, call 1-800-975-3250 (United States), or 1-800-837-5365 (Canada).

Library of Congress Cataloging-in-Publication Data

The nervous system.
pages cm. -- (Building blocks of science)
Summary: "A graphic nonfiction volume that introduces the nervous system of the human body"-- Provided by publisher.
Includes index.
ISBN 978-0-7166-1846-1
1. Nervous system--Juvenile literature.
I. World Book, Inc.
QP361.5.N46 2014
612.8--dc23
2013025431

Building Blocks of Science
ISBN: 978-0-7166-1840-9 (set, hc.)

Also available as:
ISBN: 978-0-7166-7873-1 (pbk.)
ISBN: 978-0-7166-7865-6 (trade, hc.)
ISBN: 978-0-7166-2956-6 (e-book, EPUB3)

Printed in China by Shenzhen Donnelley Printing Co., Ltd., Guangdong Province
4th printing April 2017

Acknowledgments:
Created by Samuel Hiti and Joseph Midthun
Art by Samuel Hiti
Text by Joseph Midthun
Special thanks to Syril McNally

TABLE OF CONTENTS

There is a glossary on page 30. Terms defined in the glossary are in type **that looks like this** on their first appearance.

THINKING BIG
Hello! I'm your brain.
I'm a big part of your **nervous system.**
The nervous system controls all activities in your body.
The different parts of your body must work together precisely to carry out even the simplest action.
Your nervous system coordinates all these different tasks!

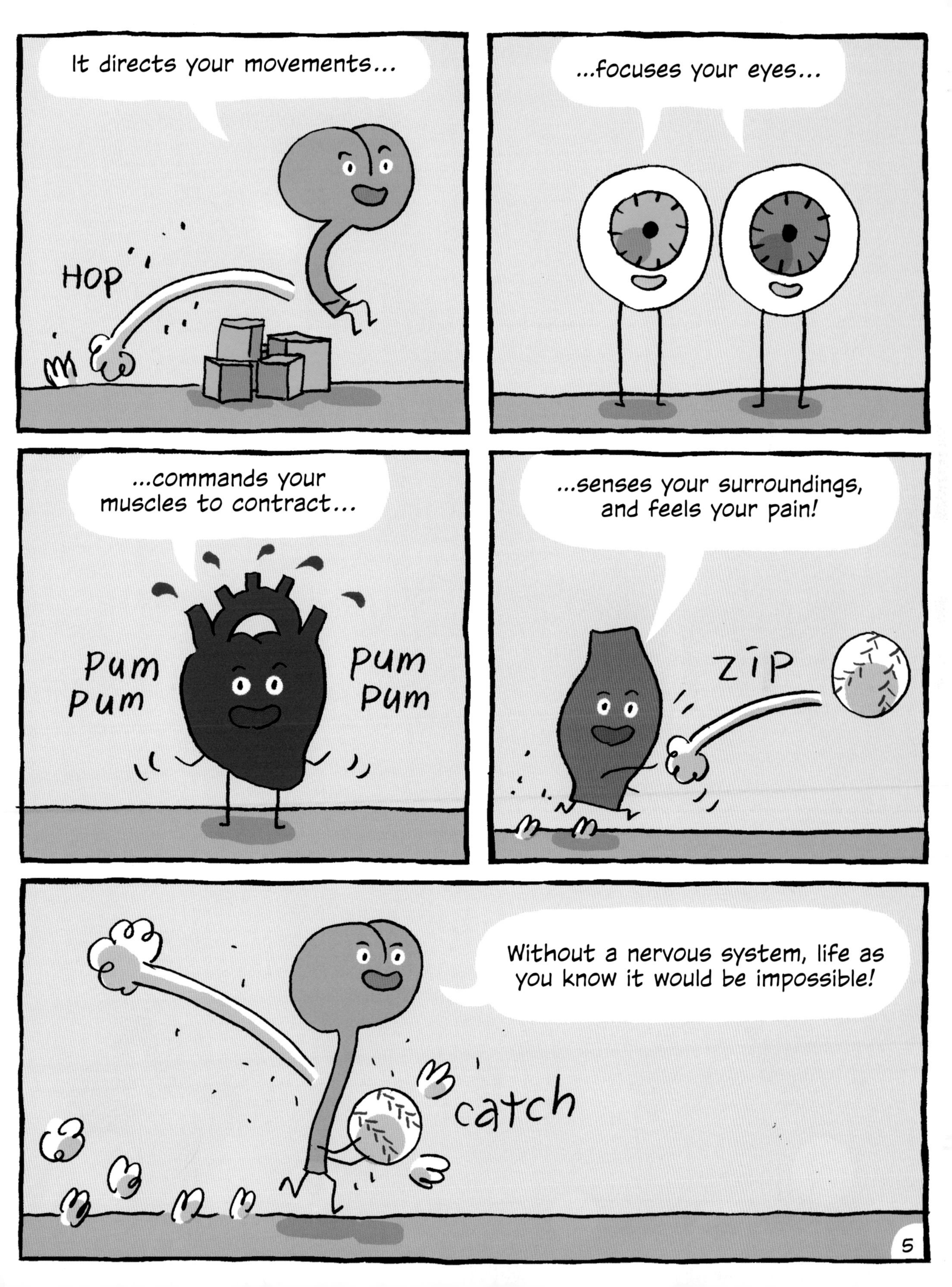
It directs your movements...
HOP
...focuses your eyes...
...commands your muscles to contract...
pum pum
pum pum
...senses your surroundings, and feels your pain!
ZIP
Without a nervous system, life as you know it would be impossible!
catch

THE NERVOUS SYSTEM
If you look really close...
...you can see that the human nervous system is made up of billions of special cells called neurons.
Neurons work together to form tissues!
Cordlike bundles of neuron fibers are called nerves.
Nerves carry messages from your sense organs, such as your eyes, ears, nose, and touch sensors in your skin.

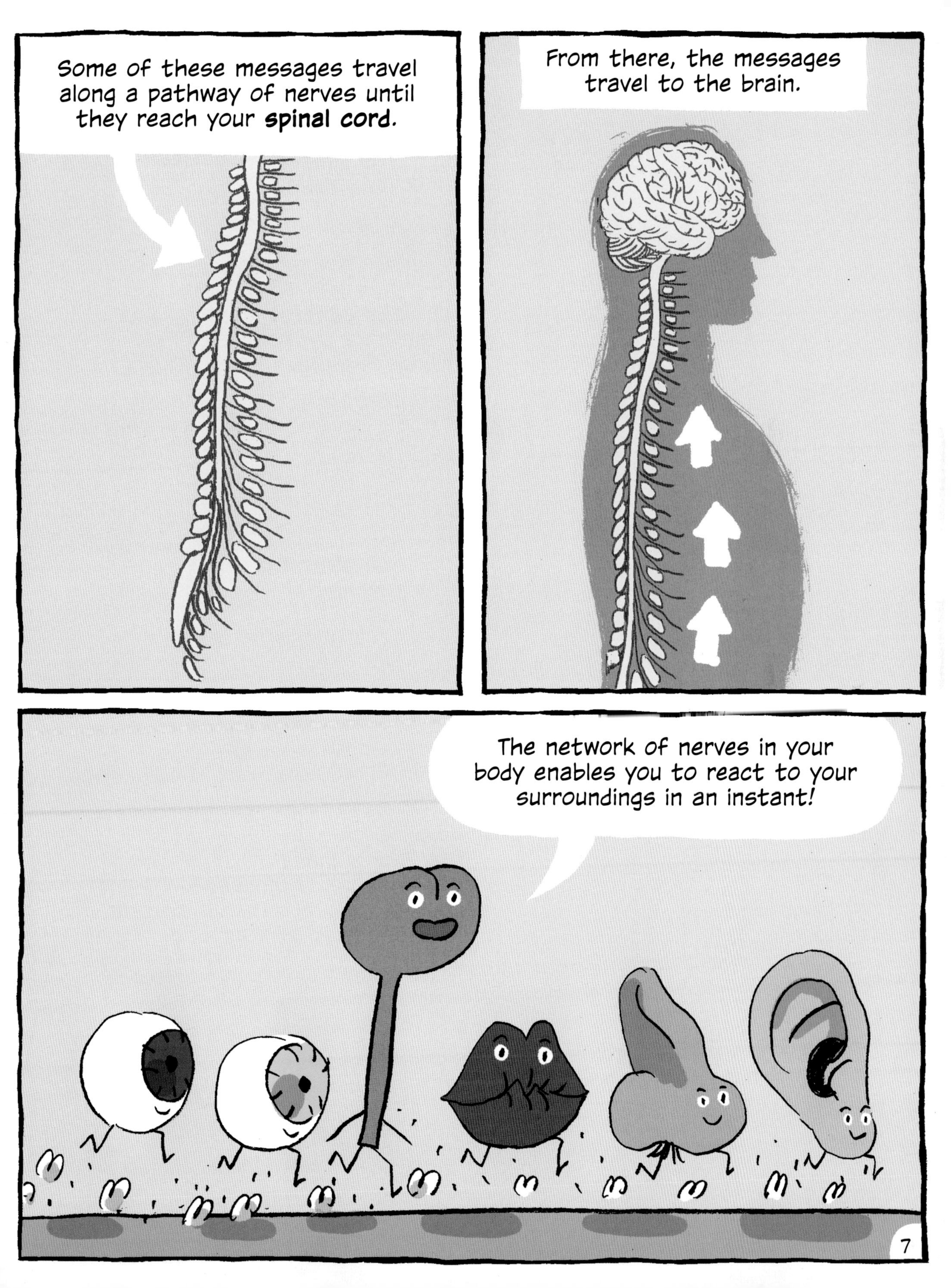
Some of these messages travel along a pathway of nerves until they reach your **spinal cord**.
From there, the messages travel to the brain.
The network of nerves in your body enables you to react to your surroundings in an instant!

PARTS OF THE NERVOUS SYSTEM

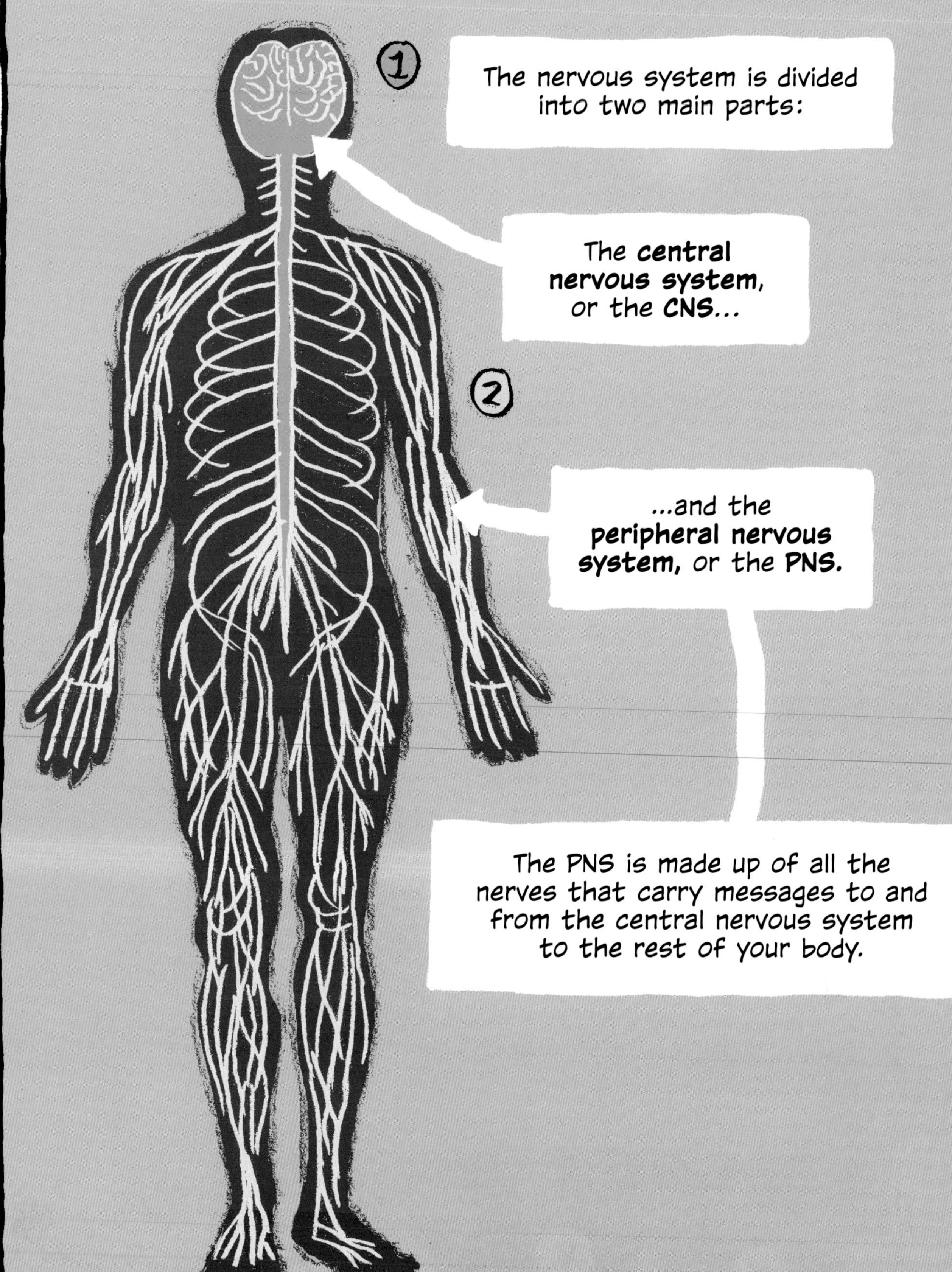

...and the PNS as the wired connection of that "computer" to all of the other parts of your body!

Let's take a closer look at how this "computer" works!

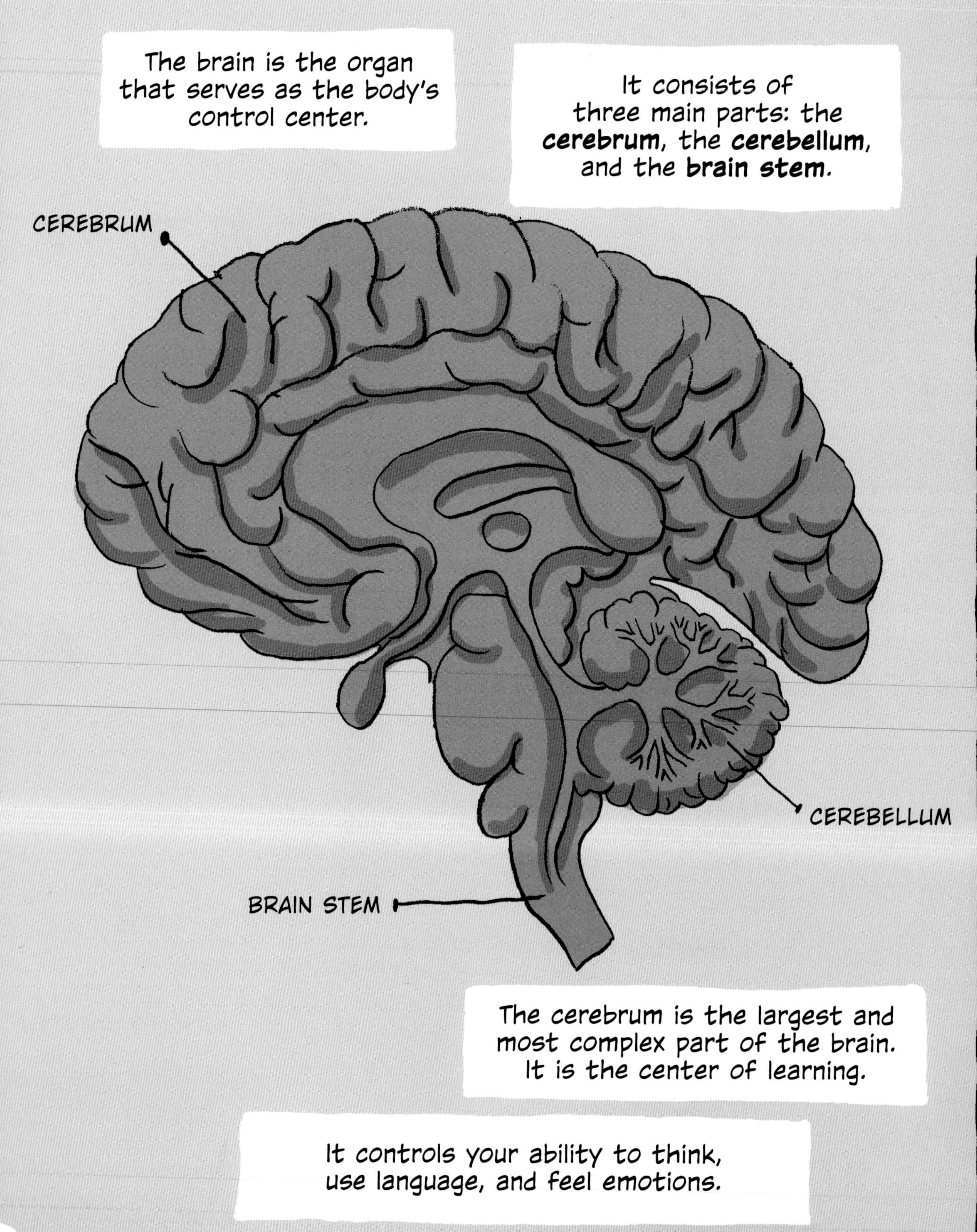
THE BRAIN
The brain is the organ that serves as the body's control center.
It consists of three main parts: the **cerebrum**, the **cerebellum**, and the **brain stem**.
CEREBRUM
CEREBELLUM
BRAIN STEM
The cerebrum is the largest and most complex part of the brain. It is the center of learning.
It controls your ability to think, use language, and feel emotions.

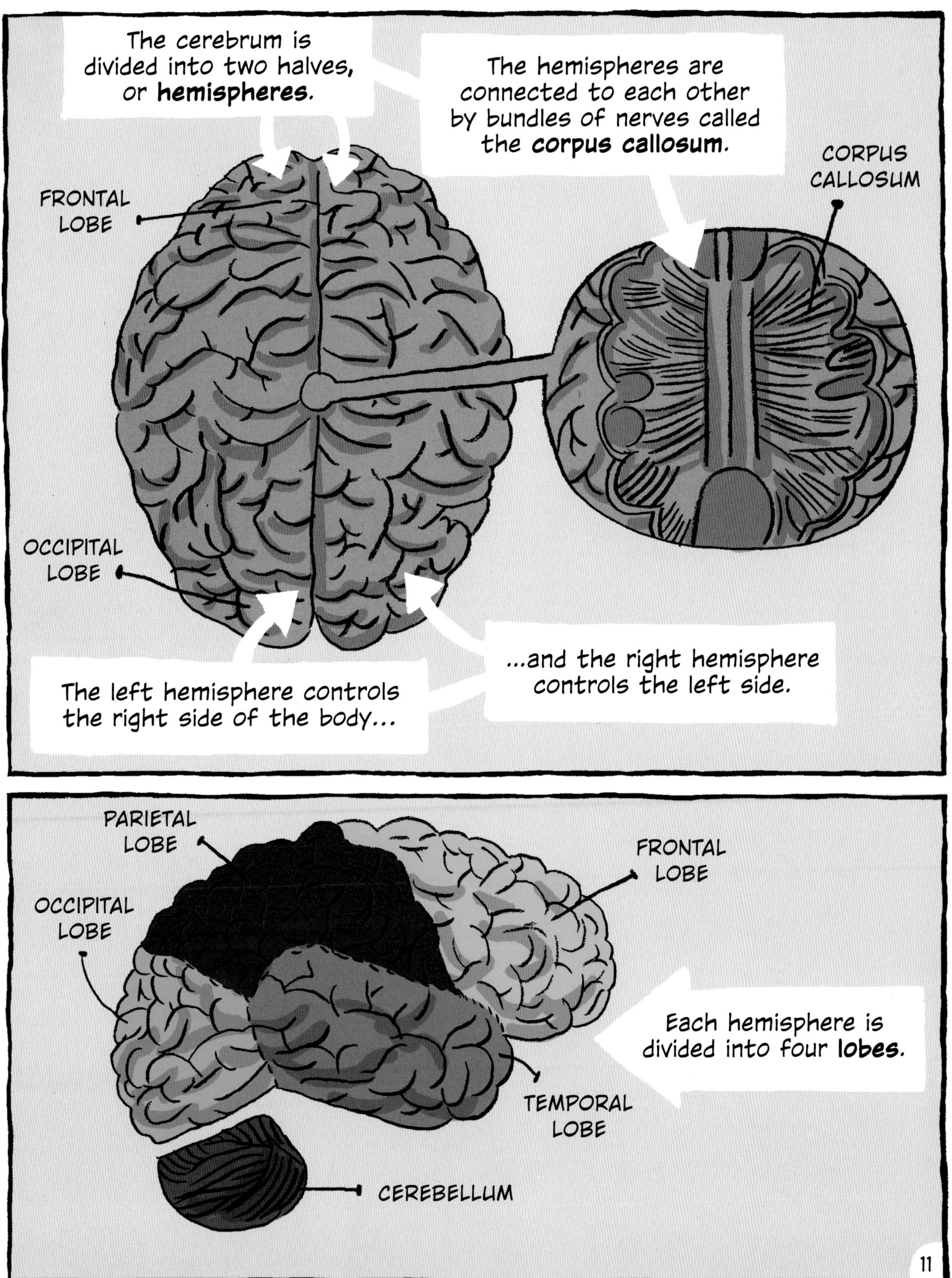
The cerebrum is divided into two halves, or **hemispheres**.
The hemispheres are connected to each other by bundles of nerves called the **corpus callosum**.
FRONTAL LOBE
CORPUS CALLOSUM
OCCIPITAL LOBE
The left hemisphere controls the right side of the body...
...and the right hemisphere controls the left side.
PARIETAL LOBE
OCCIPITAL LOBE
FRONTAL LOBE
Each hemisphere is divided into four **lobes**.
TEMPORAL LOBE
CEREBELLUM

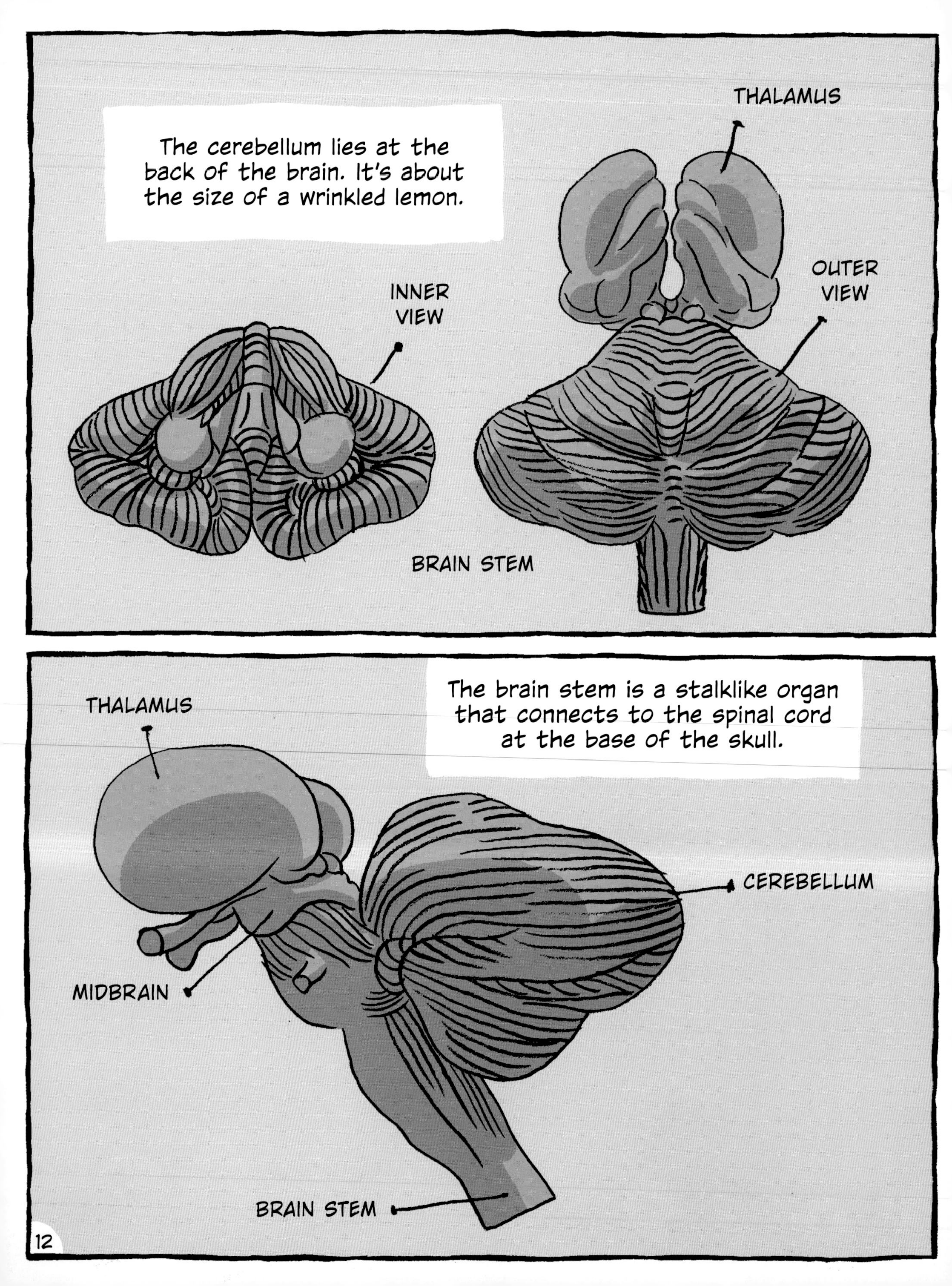
The cerebellum lies at the back of the brain. It's about the size of a wrinkled lemon.
THALAMUS
INNER VIEW
OUTER VIEW
BRAIN STEM
The brain stem is a stalklike organ that connects to the spinal cord at the base of the skull.
THALAMUS
CEREBELLUM
MIDBRAIN
BRAIN STEM

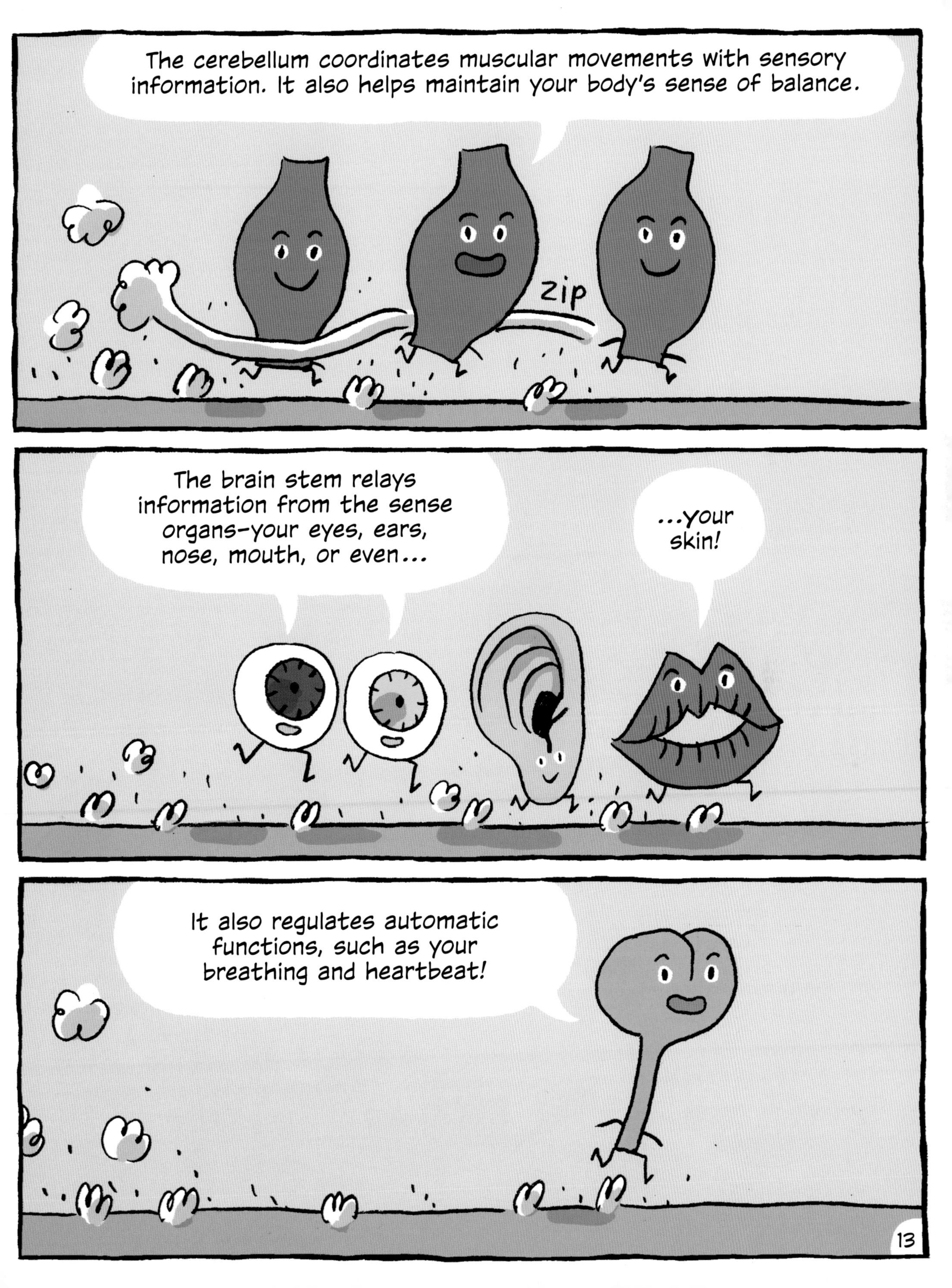
The cerebellum coordinates muscular movements with sensory information. It also helps maintain your body's sense of balance.
zip
The brain stem relays information from the sense organs—your eyes, ears, nose, mouth, or even...
...your skin!
It also regulates automatic functions, such as your breathing and heartbeat!

VOLUNTARY AND INVOLUNTARY ACTIONS
Your mind is always active.
Every second, the brain is receiving information from inside and outside the body—
—even when you are sleeping!
Your brain then decodes that information...
...decides how to respond...
...and instructs the body to do so!
WUP
WACK
But the brain doesn't just react to things.
It can also act!
WOOSH

Walking, speaking, and eating are all **voluntary actions.**
They are actions that your brain chooses to do!
Hey!
HOP
Hop
HOP
But the brain also controls many other actions that you are not aware of...
...such as blood circulation, digestion, and maintaining body temperature.
KLUNK
skid
HOP
These are **involuntary actions,** meaning, your body does them without being told.
They're automatic!
Blip
wack

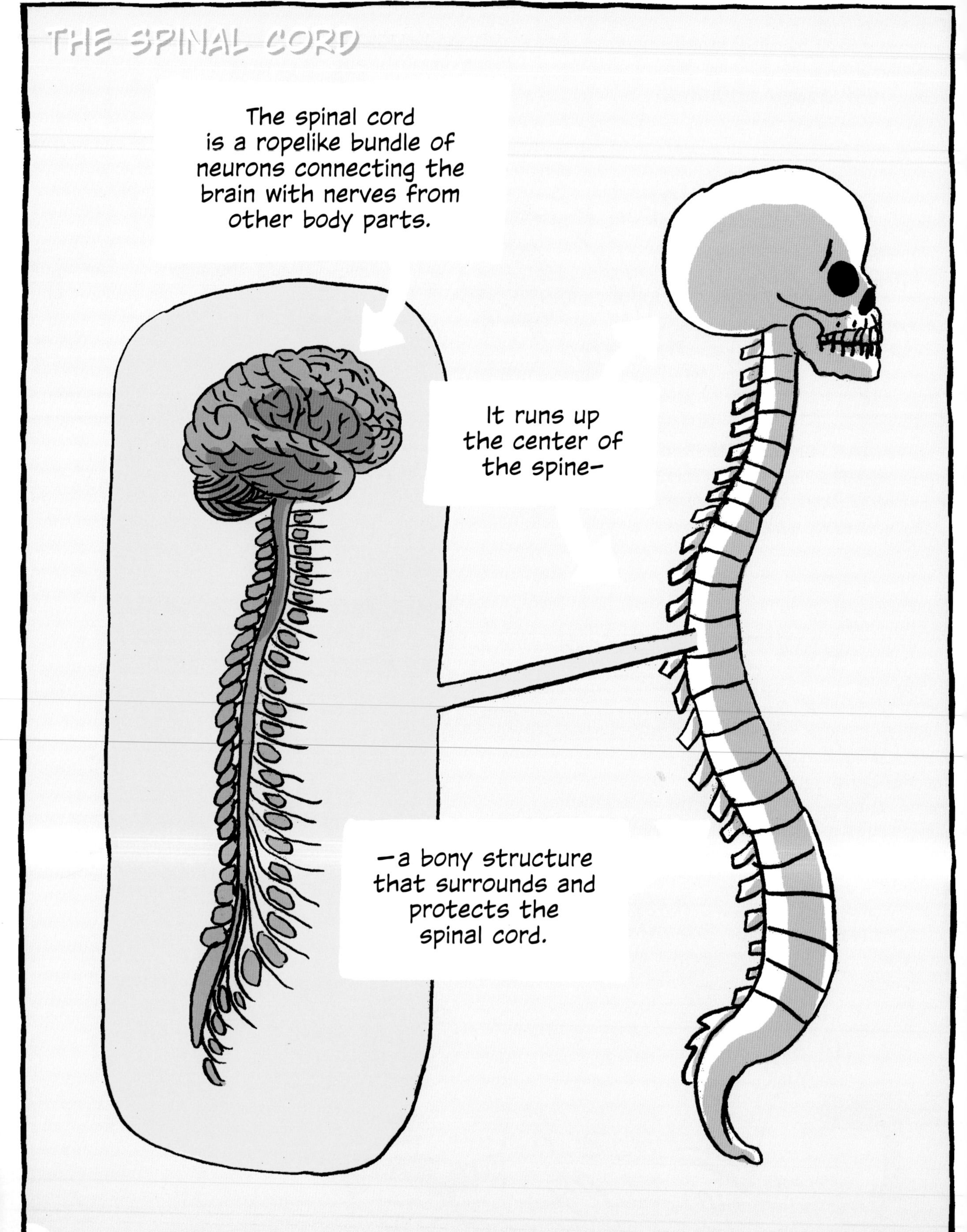
THE SPINAL CORD
The spinal cord is a ropelike bundle of neurons connecting the brain with nerves from other body parts.
It runs up the center of the spine–
–a bony structure that surrounds and protects the spinal cord.

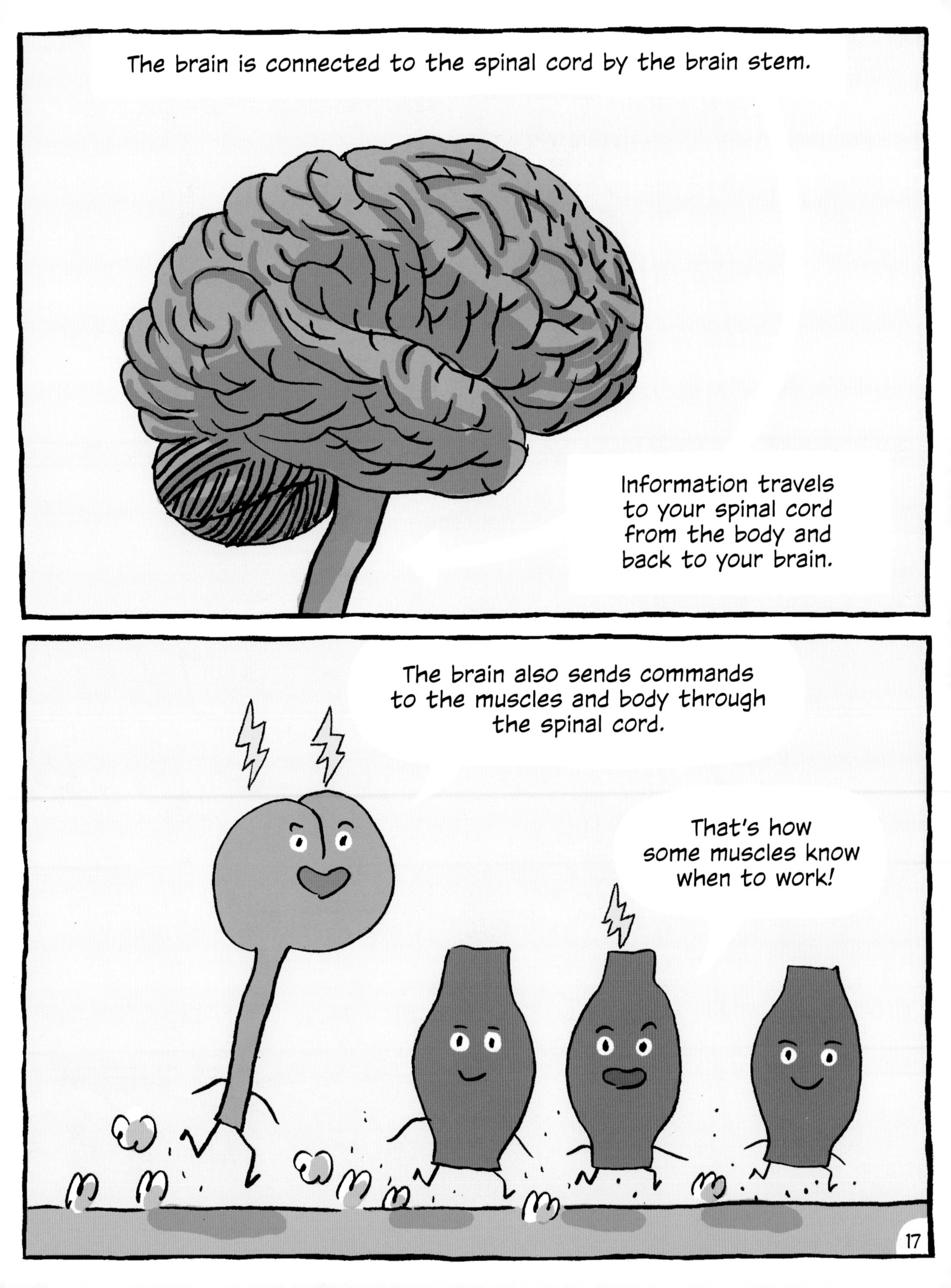
The brain is connected to the spinal cord by the brain stem.
Information travels to your spinal cord from the body and back to your brain.
The brain also sends commands to the muscles and body through the spinal cord.
That's how some muscles know when to work!

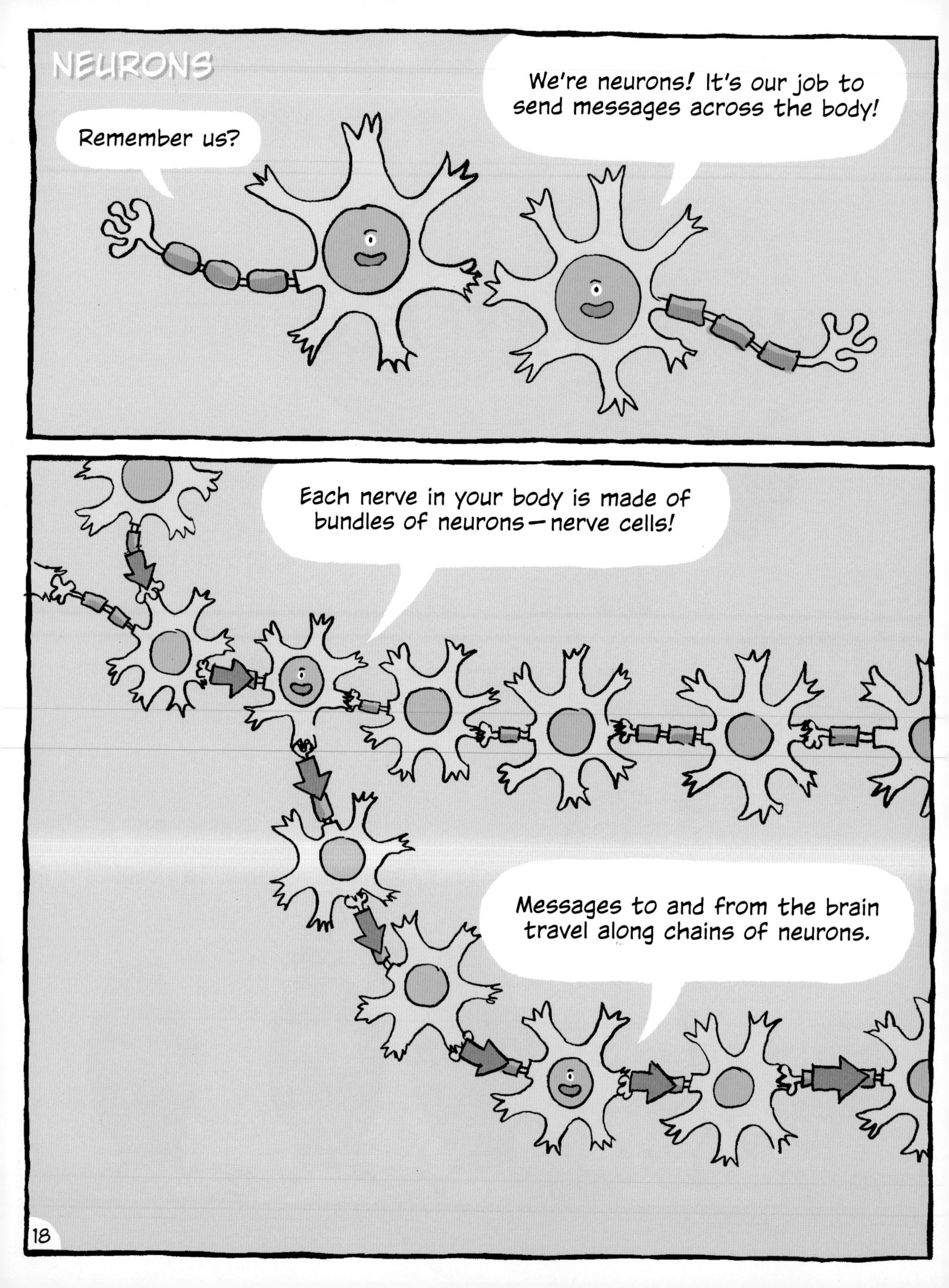
NEURONS
Remember us?
We're neurons! It's our job to send messages across the body!
Each nerve in your body is made of bundles of neurons—nerve cells!
Messages to and from the brain travel along chains of neurons.

A neuron has three basic parts: the **cell body,** the **axon,** and the **dendrites**.

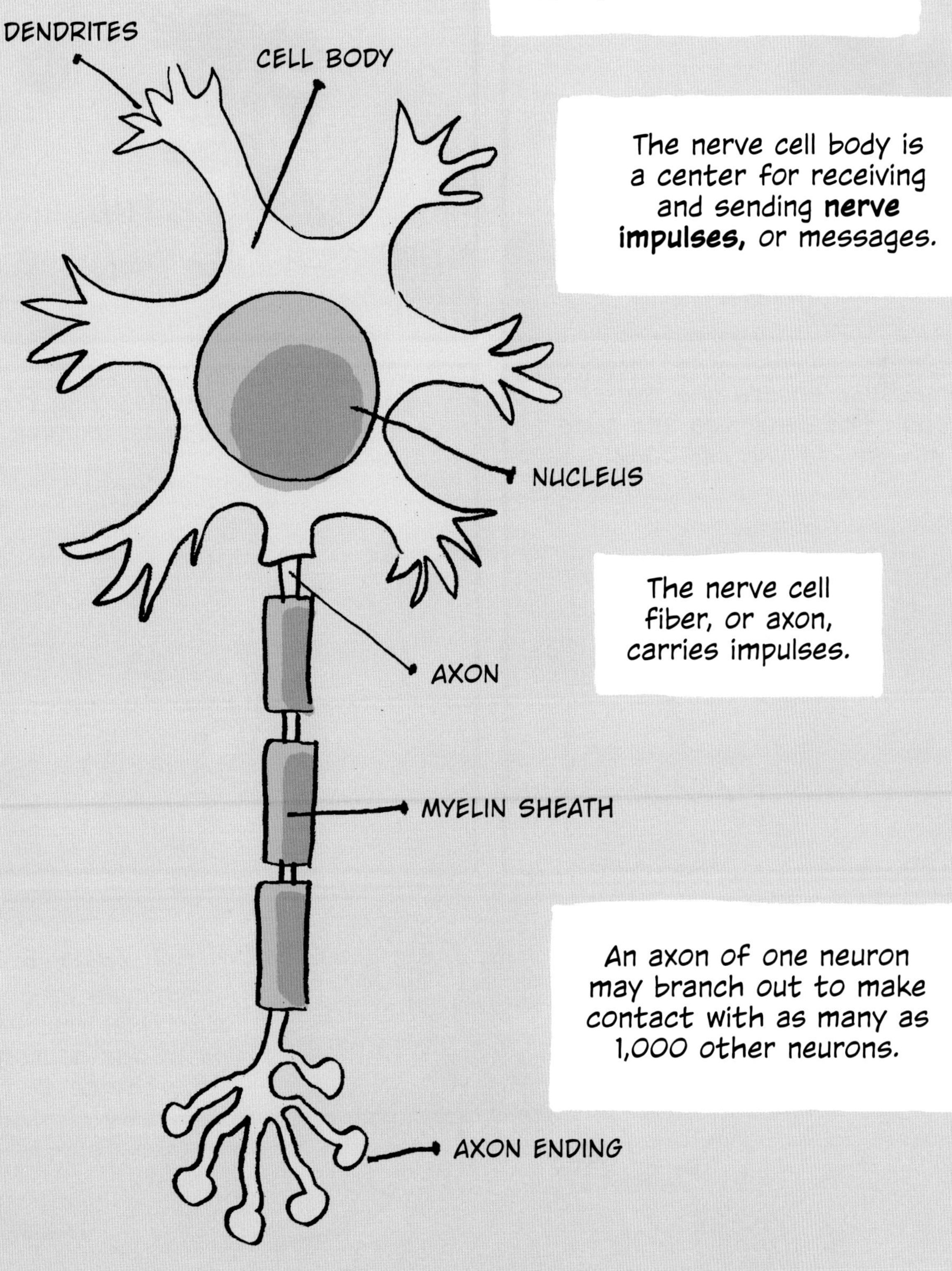

The nerve cell body is a center for receiving and sending **nerve impulses,** or messages.

The nerve cell fiber, or axon, carries impulses.

An axon of one neuron may branch out to make contact with as many as 1,000 other neurons.

FROM THE INSIDE...

You receive information from the outside world and from inside your body all the time!
stub.

A message enters the neuron through the dendrites and goes directly to the cell body.

The message travels along the axon as an electrical impulse.

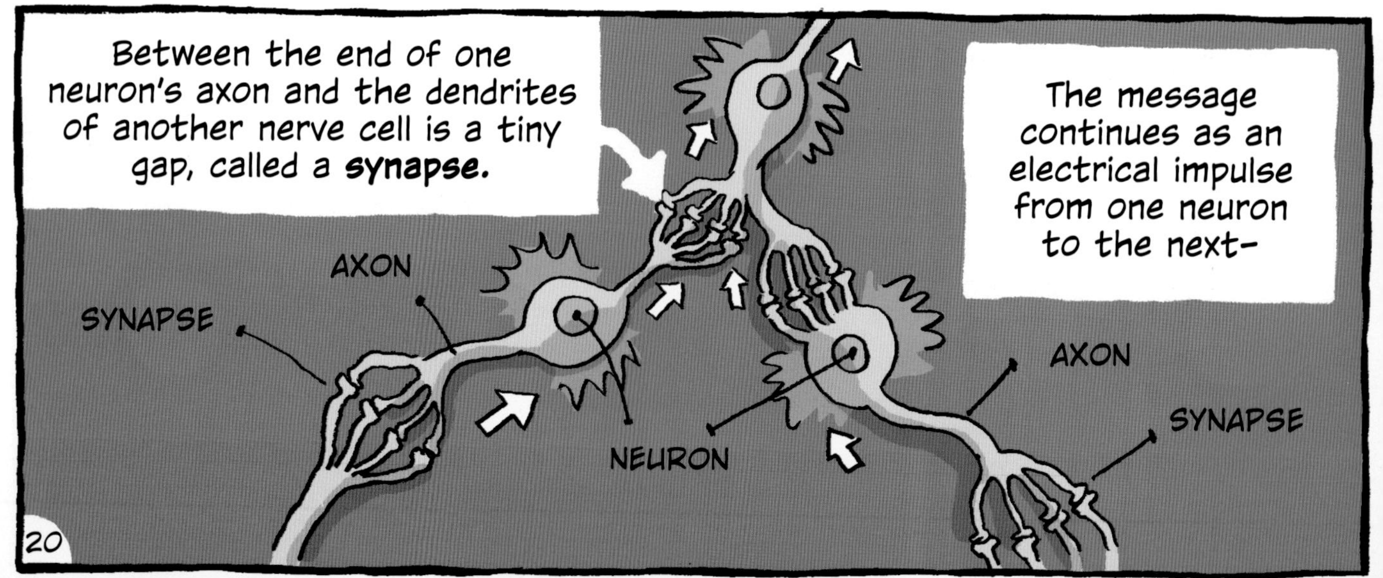
Between the end of one neuron's axon and the dendrites of another nerve cell is a tiny gap, called a **synapse.**
The message continues as an electrical impulse from one neuron to the next-
AXON
SYNAPSE
NEURON
AXON
SYNAPSE

-a chain reaction!
Urgent message coming through!
Okay, I'll pass it on!
Your neurons carry the information to your brain.
Priority message!
Thank you...
The brain then decodes the signals as a sight, sound, smell, taste, touch, or other sensation.
Hmm.
These messages move from the brain through nerves and out to the body!
Ouch!
HOP
HOP

REFLEXES
Sometimes your body needs to respond super-fast to prevent injury.
This kind of reaction is called a **reflex.**
Look out!
HOP
ZOOM
Reflexes do not involve your brain.
Instead, impulses from your sense receptors follow a neural circuit (loop) that goes through the spinal cord.
PLOP
Tapping on the tendon below the kneecap stretches the muscle there.
Tap
This action stimulates special receptors to produce an impulse.
KICK

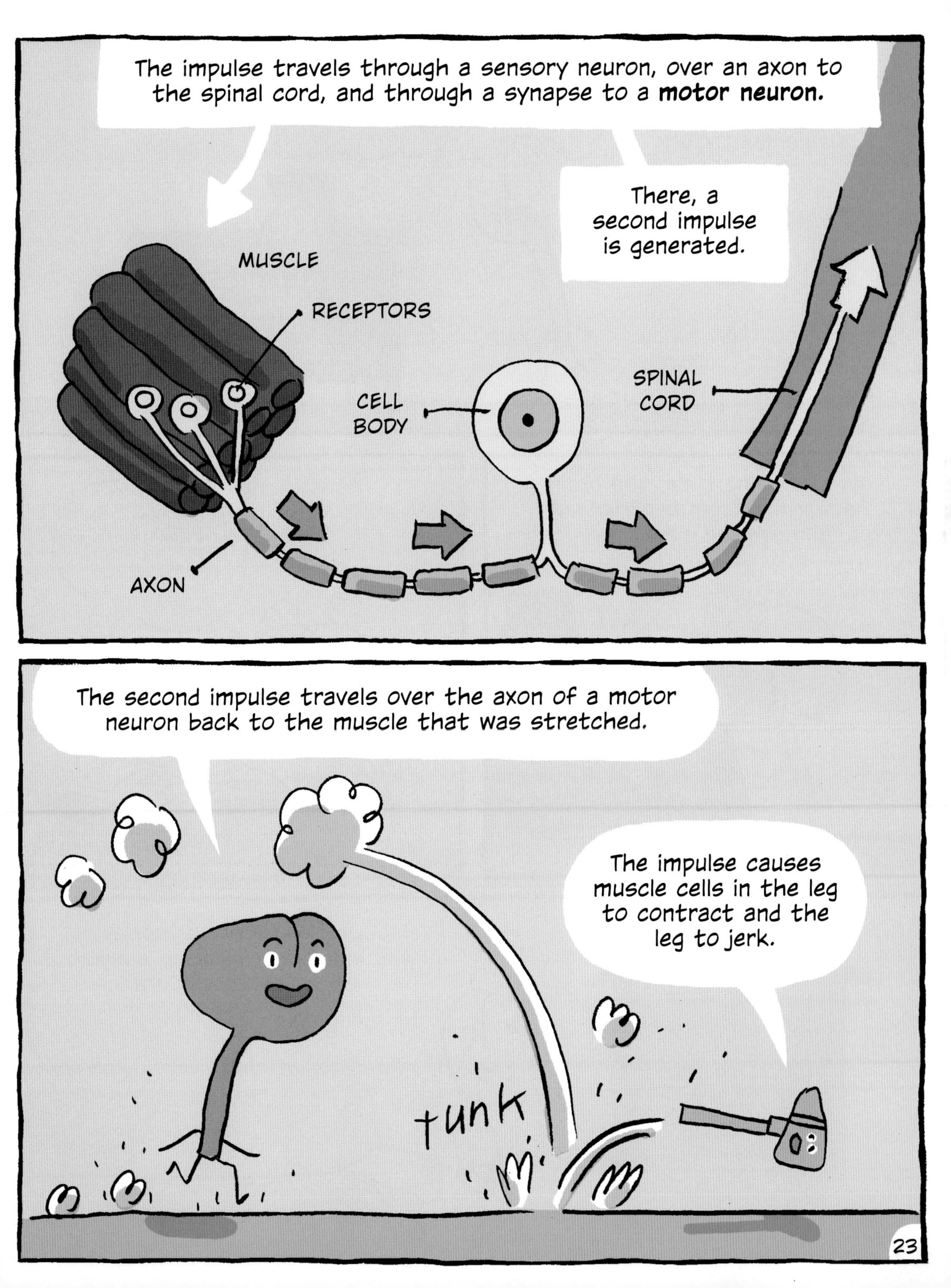
The impulse travels through a sensory neuron, over an axon to the spinal cord, and through a synapse to a **motor neuron.**
There, a second impulse is generated.
MUSCLE
RECEPTORS
CELL BODY
SPINAL CORD
AXON
The second impulse travels over the axon of a motor neuron back to the muscle that was stretched.
The impulse causes muscle cells in the leg to contract and the leg to jerk.
tunk

MEMORY AND EMOTIONS
Remember, your brain is responsible for nearly all of your actions.
Photos
Photos
Photos
At the same time, the brain is learning from experiences and storing memories!
Shif
Photos
Photos
Photos
wip
tump
Your thoughts, memories, and emotions make up a great deal of who you are.
Photos
Photos
plip

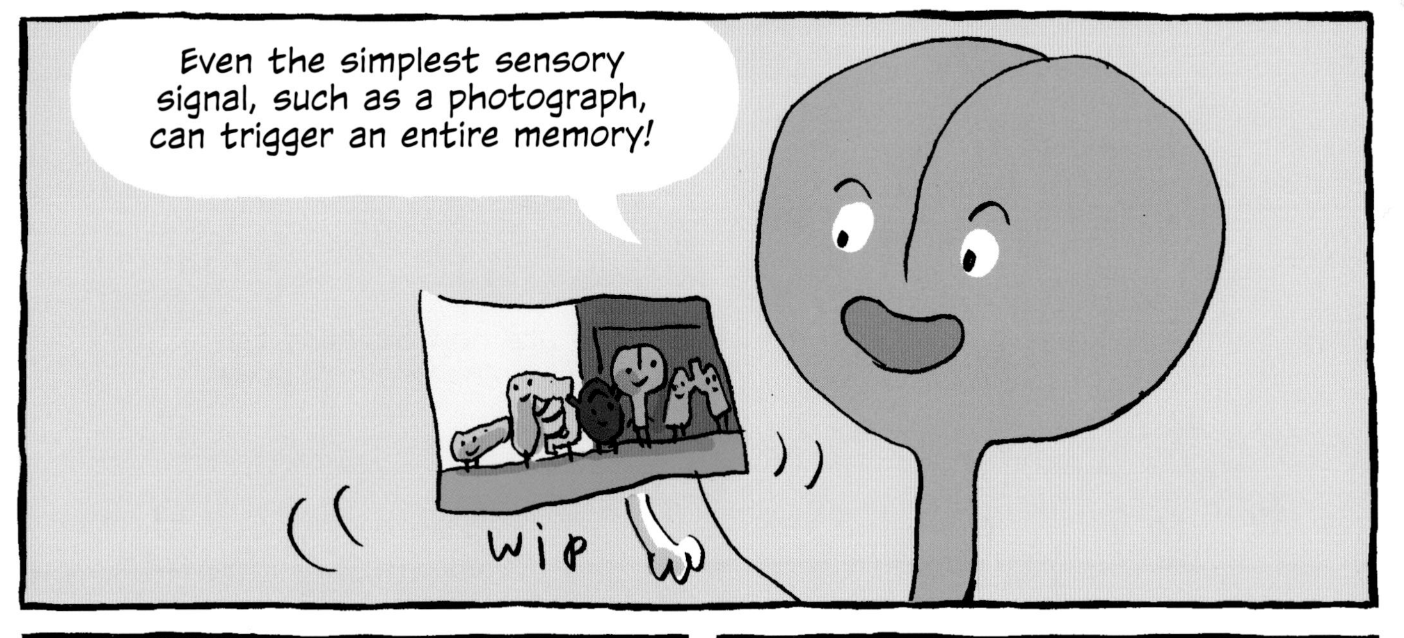

Strong emotions involve both physical responses and our understanding of what caused them.

shif

Imagine that!

MYTHS OF THE BRAIN
Scientists once believed that memories were produced and stored in separate areas of the brain.
But both are now believed to involve overlapping brain regions.
It has also been said that the left side of the brain is logical...
101
...while the right side is creative.
But it's not that simple.
Klang
Klang
Klang
In fact, as humans begin to understand their brains more and more, many myths about the brain have been debunked.
Klang
Klang
Klang

For instance, it was once believed that human beings use only 10 percent of their brain.
Nope.
We now know that *all* areas of the brain are active— if not all at the same time!
BOOP
Boop
So when you hear a statement about your brain and it doesn't seem quite right, use the scientific method-
PSH
Make a hypothesis, experiment, and check your results.
POOF
Who knows? Maybe you'll discover something new about the brain!

WONDERS OF THE BRAIN
Humans are one of the most complex organisms in the known universe.
And the nervous system is just one small part of your body!
Without it, your muscles couldn't react.
psh
PSh
Plop
You couldn't remember a tune...
...or the steps to dance to it!

Strong evidence suggests that doing activities that challenge your brain also keeps it healthy.
Makes sense to me!
Scientists have found that your brain can even grow new brain cells long into adulthood.
Remember that!
And, take another moment to ponder...
...your nervous system!

GLOSSARY

axon the tubelike structure of a neuron that carries impulses.

brain stem the part of the brain that controls information from the sense organs and involuntary actions.

cell the basic unit of all living things.

cell body the center for receiving and sending nerve impulses within a neuron.

central nervous system (CNS) part of the nervous system that includes the brain and spinal cord.

cerebellum the part of the brain that controls the coordination of muscles.

cerebrum the part of the brain that controls thoughts and voluntary actions.

corpus callosum the band of nerve fibers connecting the two hemispheres of the brain.

dendrite the branching structure of a neuron that receives impulses.

hemisphere either of the two parts that together form most of the cerebrum.

involuntary action an action that cannot be controlled by thinking.

lobe one of the four regions of the cerebrum.

motor neuron a nerve cell that carries messages to muscles.

neuron a tiny cell that sends messages across the body.

nerve a bundle of fibers that connects body parts and sends messages in the body.

nerve cell body the center for receiving and sending nerve impulses in a neuron.

nerve impulse a message carried by neurons across the body.

nervous system the group of nerves and organs that controls all activities in the body.

organ two or more tissues that work together to do a certain job.

peripheral nervous system (PNS) part of the nervous system that lies outside the brain and spinal cord.

reflex a reaction that happens without thinking.

spinal cord a group of nerves that connects the brain with the rest of the body.

synapse a place where one neuron communicates with another.

tissue a group of similar cells that do a certain job.

voluntary action an action that can be controlled by thinking.

FIND OUT MORE

Books

Human Body
by Richard Walker
(DK Children, 2009)

Human Body Factory: The Nuts and Bolts of Your Insides
by Dan Green
(Kingfisher, 2012)

Start Exploring: Gray's Anatomy: A Fact-Filled Coloring Book
by Freddy Stark
(Running Press Kids, 2011)

The Astounding Nervous System: How Does My Brain Work?
by John Burstein
(Crabtree, 2009)

The Brain: Our Nervous System
by Seymour Simon
(HarperCollins, 2006)

The Human Brain: Inside Your Body's Control Room
by Kathleen Simpson
(National Geographic Children's Books, 2009)

The Nervous System
by Christine Taylor-Butler
(Children's Press, 2008)

The Way We Work
by David Macaulay
(Houghton Mifflin/Walter Lorraine Books, 2008)

Websites

Discovery Kids: Your Nervous System
http://kids.discovery.com/tell-me/science/body-systems/your-nervous-system
Get an in-depth education on all of the parts that make up the nervous system, fun facts included!

E-Learning for Kids: Brain and Nerves
http://www.e-learningforkids.org/Courses/Liquid_Animation/Body_Parts/Brain/
Take a peek inside your brain and nerves in this clickable lesson with bonus comprehension exercises.

Kids Biology: Nervous System
http://www.kidsbiology.com/human_biology/nervous-system.php
Learn all about the nervous system by watching a short video and reading fact-filled articles complete with images of the body's organs.

Kids Health: How the Body Works
http://kidshealth.org/kid/htbw/
Select a body part to watch a video, play a word find, or read an article to learn more about its function in the human body.

National Geographic Kids: Your Amazing Brain
http://kids.nationalgeographic.com/kids/stories/spacescience/brain/
Examine a diagram of the brain while learning key facts about your body's control center.

NeoK12: Nervous System
http://www.neok12.com/Nervous-System.htm
Watch videos that illustrate the flow of the nervous system, and then take grade-specific quizzes to test your knowledge.

Science Kids: Human Body for Kids
http://www.sciencekids.co.nz/humanbody.html
Sample a range of educational games, challenging experiments, and mind-bending quizzes all while learning about human body topics.

INDEX